The Knife and Fork

The Knife and Fork

Simple Cooking

Lewis O'Neal

iUniverse, Inc.
Bloomington

THE KNIFE AND FORK
Simple Cooking

iUniverse books may be ordered through booksellers or by contacting:

iUniverse
1663 Liberty Drive
Bloomington, IN 47403
www.iuniverse.com
1-800-Authors (1-800-288-4677)

ISBN: 978-1-4759-7345-7 (sc)
ISBN: 978-1-4759-7346-4 (ebk)

Printed in the United States of America

iUniverse rev. date: 01/30/2013

Intro

My wife is such a bad cook that she makes toast with bones in it; quote by the late great Rodney Dangerfield. (By the way just for the record my wife really can cook.) Well if you happened to be one of those types of cooks, or one that is apprehensive about cooking, or one that is just starting out. Then this book is recommended for you. It has some simple basic dishes that you can make to get you comfortable with preparing meals. I know how daunting of a task it can be in trying to create something eatable without burning up half the place. I've been cooking most of my life and feel that the kitchen is the best room in the house for me. Whether I'm creating a simple sandwich or an extravagant dish. I feel that most of my creative ideas are spurred from the kitchen while I'm creating something. I feel that there is more to life than T.V. dinners and microwavable quick fixes. That's one of the lessons that I've taught to my oldest daughter who is about to start out on her own. So I started to show her some easy quick fix dishes that she could prepare without a whole lot of hassle. After some time she has become a little more comfortable with being in the kitchen and preparing her own meals. So I thought that maybe there are some concerned parents, guardians, or just some inquisitive minds that want to learn some simple things about cooking. Hopefully this will help inspire you all to take the first steps on your journey of becoming the cook that you have envisioned yourself being. I thank you for your support.

A Good Gumbo Seasoning

2 tbsp. Minced basil

2 tbsp. Minced oregano

2 tbsp. Cajun seasoning

1 tbsp. Crushed red pepper

1 tbsp. Black pepper

1 tbsp. Garlic powder

1 tbsp. Onion powder

1 tbsp. Jerk seasoning

Put all ingredients in a bowl and mix until all are well blended.

A Great Rib Rub

2 tbsp. Of smoked paprika or regular kind

2 tbsp. Black pepper

2 tbsp. Brown sugar

2 tbsp. of seasoned meat tenderizer

2 tbsp. Of dried mustard seeds

1 ½ tbsp. Red pepper

2 tbsp. Of minced fresh basil

2 tbsp. Of garlic powder

2 tbsp. Of onion powder

1 cup of honey

Juice of one lemon

In a bowl mix all the spices together, and stir until there all well blended.

Rinse your ribs off, pat partially dry, and rub both sides with honey. Coat one side with spices and rub into the meat getting in between each bone. Flip the rib over and do the same for the other side. Cut lemon in half, using a fork poke several holes into the open end of the lemons. Use a small strainer to catch the seeds of the lemon, squeeze the juice out of the lemon into the strainer drizzle over one side of the rib. Repeat for the other side with the other half of lemon. Put rib in container cover and put in frig let set for 24hrs. Before cooking ribs let sit out for 1 ½ hours or till it gets to room temp.

Homemade Garden Salsa

1 ½ Tomatoes diced
1 medium green bell pepper diced
1 jalapeno seeded and diced
1 tbsp. minced garlic
1 tbsp. crushed red pepper
2 cilantro leaves minced
1 can sweet yellow corn drained
1 can black beans drained and rinsed
1 tbsp. fresh minced basil
1 medium sweet yellow onion diced
3 spinach leaves finely minced
1 tbsp. fresh oregano

Directions:

Mix all ingredients and serve.

Easy Make You Cry Hot Sauce

Ingredients:

1 cup of tomatoes sauce
1 tbsp. Of apple cider vinegar
1 ½ tbsp. Sugar
1 habanero pepper finely diced
1 jalapeno pepper finely diced
1 tbsp. Chili pepper
1 teaspoon crushed red pepper
1 tbsp. Smoked paprika
2 teaspoons sea salt
2 teaspoons of coarse grind black pepper
¼ cup of orange juice

Directions:

Put all ingredients in cooking pot and cook on medium high heat. Using a whisk stir while cooking. Cook until sugar is all the way dissolved. Pour into Mason jar and let cool. After 24hr. It is ready to serve.

Burger Dressing

1 tea spoon lemon juice

1 teaspoon honey

1 tbsp. Minced basil

¼ cup Russian dressing

¼ cup mayo or miracle whip light

1 teaspoon fresh cracked peppercorns

1 teaspoon crushed red pepper

Put all ingredients in a bowl and whisk together, until all are well blended. Cover and refrigerate for 30 min. Serve

(Optional) Top burgers with a sharp cheddar, or aged Gouda cheese, for a zesty, zingy taste.

Spinach Dip

1-can spinach (drained) or frozen thawed and squeezed dry
1 tomato diced
4 strips of bacon fully cooked and crumbled
½ cup crumbled blue cheese crumbles
½ cup season dry bread crumbs
½ cup grated parmasean cheese
¼ cup shredded mozzarella
¼ cup diced onion

Put spinach in paper towel and squeeze dry. In a bowl combine dry season breadcrumbs, and grated parmesan then set aside. In casserole dish combine spinach, blue cheese, diced tomatoes, onions, shredded mozzarella, and crumbled bacon. Thoroughly mix all together top with breadcrumb mixture. Put in oven at 350 for 25 min. once cheese is melted all the way through it is ready to serve.

Chicken Nacho Dip

1 can nacho cheese

1 diced tomatoes

¼ cup minced cilantro

1 diced jalapeno seeded

¼ cup diced onion

1 lb. chorizo

1 cup fully cooked shredded chicken

1 tbs. Chopped garlic

¼ cup olive oil

In a skillet heat olive oil then add onion, and chopped garlic. Sauté until onions and garlic starts to brown then add chorizo. Cook the chorizo all the way through stirring constantly. Drain of access grease then pat dry. In a microwaveable safe bowl add all the other remaining ingredients and mix well. Microwave on high for 4 to 5 min. Serve. Top with sour cream and chopped green onions.

Sweet Potato Fry Dip

2 tbsp. Sour cream

1 tbsp. Honey

1 teaspoon light brown sugar

1 teaspoon sugar

1 teaspoon syrup

Mix all ingredients together stir until well blended

Easy Quick Fix Honey Mustard

Ingredients:

1 cup Deion mustard
½ cup honey
½ cup mayo
1 teaspoon lemon pepper
1 teaspoon light brown sugar

Combine all ingredients in a bowl stir until blended. Serve.

Sweet Heat Mustard Base BBQ Sauce

1 tbsp. Cayenne pepper
1 ½ cups Dijon Mustard
1 sprig of Rosemary
1 sprig of Thyme
1 tbsp. light brown sugar
1/3 cup Maple Syrup
¼ cup Honey
¼ cup Apple Cider Vinegar
1 shot of Tequila
¼ cup sliced Green Onions

Directions:

Put all ingredients in a pot and let simmer over medium low heat. Let simmer 10 to 15 minutes. Constantly stirring until sauce starts to boil. Remove from heat let sauce thicken. Serve.

White Peppercorn Gravy

1-cup all-purpose flour
½-cup heavy cream
½-cup milk
1-tlbs minced garlic
1-tlbs. Minced onions
2-tlbs. Butter

In non-stick skillet heat butter then add onions, and minced garlic. Sauté until onions are soft then add flour stirring until start to thicken. Add heavy cream and milk stirring until it starts to boil. Reduce heat add crushed peppercorns and constantly stir until sauce becomes thick and creamy. Serve.

Chilled Fruit Parfait

½ cup strawberry glaze
1 cup diced cantaloupe
1 cup diced honeydew
½ cup diced strawberries
3 bananas peeled and sliced
1/3 cup sun dried raisins
2 cups of cool whip
1 cup of crunched up honey nut clusters cereal
1 cinnamon stick

Take a couple of ice cream glasses and put them in the freezer until their frozen. Or 3 to 4 hours.

In a large bowl, combine all fruits and strawberry glaze, using a grater. Grate cinnamon stick over top of fruit.

Cover the bowl and shake until all fruit is well blended.

Spoon one layer of fruit mixture into bottom of chilled ice cream glass, followed by two spoons of cool whip. Repeat process until glass is almost full. With the last level of cool whip top off with crunched up honey nut cluster cereal.

The New Fruit Salsa

Ingredients:

1 cup diced Strawberries

1 cup diced Pineapples

1 sweet green granny smith apple peeled and diced

1 mint leaf finely chopped

1 cup diced Cantaloupe

¾ cup freshly squeezed orange juice

½ cup yellow raisins (optional)

½ cup sliced Cherries

Directions:

Mix all ingredients in a large bowl. Cover tightly with foil or plastic wrap. Refrigerate 2 to 3 hours. Best served chilled.

Tropical Coleslaw

Ingredients:

1 head red cabbage shredded
1 head green cabbage shredded
1 head iceberg lettuce shredded
1 cup shredded carrots
½ cup shredded coconut
Juice of 1 lemon
1 red bell pepper diced
1 yellow bell pepper diced
1 green bell pepper diced
1 sweet yellow onion diced
1 tbsp. fresh ground peppercorns
1 tsp. all spice
½ cup diced pineapples
½ cup mayo light

Directions:

Put all ingredients except lemon juice in a large bowl and toss until well blended together. Once well blended drizzle lemon juice over top and toss lightly, cover and refrigerate for 2-3 hours. Serve chilled

Stuffed Jalapeno Peppers

1 package (8 oz. cream cheese soften)
1 cup of diced cooked chicken
15 jalapeno peppers
1 cup shredded part-skim mozzarella cheese
1 cup taco sauce
1 cup of grated parmasean
1 cup of season dried bread crumbs

In a bowl combine bread crumbs and grated parmasean, using your hands mix the two. Cut jalapeno's in half discard the seeds. Stuff jalapenos with chicken, cream cheese, and mozzarella. Once their stuffed pour taco sauce over the top of each one, then sprinkle each with the bread crumb mixture. Greases a baking dish with 1/3 cup of olive oil. Place jalapeno's in dish and bake uncovered on 350 for 20 to 25 min. or till cheese is melted all the way through and the bread crumbs is a golden brown color. Serve

South Of the Boarder Baked Beans

½ cup diced green pepper
½ cup diced yellow pepper
½ cup diced red pepper
1 cup sliced green onions
½ cup diced jalapenos
1 cup sweet yellow corn
1/3 cup chopped cilantro
1 cup light brown sugar
2 tbs. Minced garlic
1 lb. chorizo
1 can bush's baked beans
1 can of black beans rinsed and drained
Juice of one lime

Cook Chorizo until lightly browned then drain. Combine all ingredients and Chorizo into baking dish. Make sure all ingredients are well mixed. Cover dish and bake at 350 for about 45-50 minutes. When finished uncover and let sit for 10 minutes then serve.

Chicken Grilled Cheese

1 slice cheddar cheese
1-slice Swiss cheese
½ stick butter
½ cup diced chicken breast fully cooked
1-tlbs minced pepperoni
1-tlbs. Minced onion
A pinch of fresh minced dill

In a bowl mix chicken, pepperoni, minced onion, and dill. Once mixed layer your bread with Swiss cheese, chicken mixture, sliced cheddar, then next layer of bread. In a nonstick skillet melt butter then add sandwich. Cook 2 min. per side or until browned on both sides and cheese in between is well melted through. Serve.

Chicken Vegetable Soup

1 cup chopped carrots
1 cup diced red potatoes
1 cup snow peas
1 cup pearl onions
2 cups chicken broth
2 cups vegetable stock
1 cup chopped celery
4 bay leafs
¼ cup minced basil
1 ½ cups cooked chicken strip
1 tbs. Minced garlic
1 tbs. all spice

In a large crock-pot combine all ingredients and cook on low for 5 to 6 hours. Serve

Chili Explosion

½ diced jalapenos

1 cup diced green peppers

1 cup diced yellow peppers

1 can sweet corn

1 can of black beans drained and rinsed

¼ cup cumin

1/3 cup sweet paprika

1 cup diced sweet yellow onions

1 cup diced red onions

¼ cup crushed roasted garlic

1 lb. ground sirloin

1 lb. fresh ground spicy Italian sausage

1 can hot chili beans

½ cup chili powder

1 can tomato paste

1 can diced tomato's

1 can stew tomatoes

1/3 cup hot chili oil

1 cup sugar

1 cup beer

In a large deep dish skillet heat ¼ cup olive oil and add green peppers, yellow peppers, red and yellow onions. Cook until they become tender and then add Italian sausage, and ground sirloin. Cook until meat starts to brown lightly, and then drain of access grease. Add meat mixture along with all other remaining ingredients. Stir and cook covered on medium low heat for 3 ½ hours.

Breakfast Casserole

Ingredients:

3 large potatoes peeled and thinly shredded
1 lb. chorizo sausage
1 green pepper diced
1 red pepper diced
1 onion diced
1 diced jalapeno pepper
½ cup pepper jack cheese shredded
½ cup Colby cheese shredded
3 large eggs
1 tomato diced
2 tbsp. olive oil
2 tbsp. chopped basil

Directions:

Heat oil in a skillet until medium hot, once oil is hot add diced potatoes, green pepper, red pepper onions, and diced jalapeno. Cook until potatoes are fork tender, with occasional stirring. In separate skillet brown chorizo sausage. Drain both skillet of excess grease. In a bowl beat eggs until whipped. Spray bottom of Casserole dish with cooking spray. Combine ingredients in both skillets in casserole dish and mix. Pour whipped eggs on top and add diced tomato, chopped basil, both shredded cheeses and mix all together. Cover dish, place in oven on 350° for 20 to 25 minutes or until eggs have risen. Once done take out of oven let sit for 10 minutes. Serve (topping optional recommend homemade garden salsa)

Easy Tuna Casserole

12 0z. Bag of no yolk egg noodles
1 cup of frozen peas
2 cans of tuna drained
½ of a diced onion
1 can cream of celery
1 can of Campbell's cheddar cheeses
1 cup of shredded cheese of your choice
1 ¼ cups of mayo (I prefer miracle whip light with olive oil)

In a casserole dish combine tuna, cream of celery, can of cheddar cheese, and mayo. Boil egg noodles per package directions, then drain and rinse. Add to mixture along with frozen peas. Top with shredded cheese. Cover and bake 25-30 min. at 350.

Oven Fried Chicken

Ingredients:

1 quart of buttermilk
2 cups flour
1 tbsp. Cayenne pepper
2 tbsp. Light brown sugar
1 tbsp. Minced thyme
1 tbsp. Minced rosemary
3 lbs. assorted chicken pieces wings, legs, breast, and thighs.
2 cups of finely crushed corn flakes

In a large bowl, combine chicken, buttermilk, salt and pepper. Cover and let set in refrigerator overnight. Season flour with rosemary, thyme, and light brown sugar. Coat chicken with the flour mixture shaking off the access flour. Dip back into buttermilk, then coat with cornflakes. In a cast iron skillet coat bottom with 1/3 cup extra virgin olive oil. Bake at 350, for 30-45 min. or until chicken is no longer pink on the inside. (Turn chicken over after the first 10-12 min. of cooking.) Place back into oven and let cook the rest of the way through.

Loaded Baked Potatoes Salad

1 cup honey Dijon mustard

1 medium-diced onion

1 cup light mayo

8 pieces of fully cooked crumbled maple bacon

½ cup sweet pickle relish

10 red potatoes

2 tbsp. Sugar

2 tbsp. Ms. Dash southwest seasoning

¼ cup extra virgin olive oil

Add a pinch of smoked paprika and dill

1 Green bell pepper diced and seeded

Cut red potatoes in half and put into large bowl. Season with Ms. Dash southwest seasoning, and drizzle with olive oil. Add onion and green pepper, and toss. Add to baking dish cover with foil and bake at 350 for 45 to 55 min. or until potatoes become fork tender. Put in a large bowl and add all remaining ingredients and mix. Cover and refrigerate for 3 to 4 hours. Serve.

Baked Spaghetti and Homemade Sauce

Ingredients:

1 box of spaghetti noodles
½ cup Grated Parmesan cheese
½ cup dried seasoned bread crumbs
1 ½ lbs. lean ground beef or ground chuck
2 tbsp. crushed garlic
1 lb. lean crisp bacon fully cooked and crumbled
2 tbsp. fresh minced basil
2 tbsp. fresh mince oregano
½ cup diced red onion
1 cup of shredded mozzarella cheese
1 cup of shredded white cheddar
1 can (2 ¼ ounces) sliced black olives, drained and chopped (optional)

Sauce Ingredients:

1 can (14.5 oz.) diced tomatoes with basil, garlic and oregano
1 cup red wine
½ tbsp. Minced garlic
½ cup sugar
1 tbsp. crushed red pepper
1 can hunts tomato sauce (garlic and herb)

Directions:

In a saucepan, combine all sauce ingredients. Cook on medium low, stirring a couple of minutes to prevent sticking. Reduce heat once bubbling starts. Whole process should take 10-15 minutes.

Cook spaghetti noodle per box directions, meanwhile brown ground beef or chuck add oregano, basil, onions, crushed garlic to meat while cooking. Drain excess grease. In casserole dish, add ground beef or chuck mixture and spaghetti noodles, black olives and shredded mozzarella and white cheddar, mix all together. Now add sauce and mix. Sprinkle crumbled bacon across the top. In a separate bowl, add seasoned bread crumbs and parmesan, then sprinkle mixture across top starting with corners. Cover and bake on 350 for 15 minutes and then uncover and bake additional 10 minutes. Once done let sit for 5-10 minutes before serving.

Note:

If you don't have bread crumbs you can substitute crushed salad croutons instead.

Shredded Chicken Nacho's

3 cooked chicken breast

1 can of nacho cheese

1 cup of shredded extra sharp cheddar cheese

1 cup sliced jalapenos

1 can black beans drained and rinsed

1 jar of medium salsa

¼ cup of minced garlic

¼ cup of minced cilantro

1 can of sweet corn drained

1 small diced sweet red pepper

1 small diced sweet yellow pepper

1 package of taco seasoning

¼ cup of lime juice

½ cup diced onions

¼ cup extra virgin olive oil

Using two forks pull and shred chicken apart. Heat olive oil in skillet on medium high heat. Once oil is heated add shredded chicken, taco seasoning, onions, lime juice, red and yellow peppers, sweet corn, garlic, cilantro, and black beans. Mix all together and cook till onions, and peppers are tender. Drain chicken mixture of access grease. In a round casserole dish fill with nacho chips, or tortilla chips. Top with shredded extra sharp cheddar cheese, chicken mixture, nacho cheese, sliced jalapenos, and salsa. Place in oven at 350 bake till cheese is melted. Garnish with a spoon full of sour cream, 1/3 cup diced green onions, and chives.

Chicken and Spinach Stromboli

1 cup pizza sauce

1 cup shredded mozzarella cheese

1 cup diced pepperoni

¼ minced garlic

½ cup melted butter

½ cup minced sweet basil

½ cup oregano

8 slices of provolone cheese

1 cup of shredded cooked chicken breast

1 cup of baby leaf spinach

Directions:

Add Oregano, basil, minced garlic and butter to a cup then melt. Once melted sit to the side. Next flour surface (helps prevent pizza dough from tearing and sticking to surface). Roll out pizza dough with rolling pin. Once rolled out cut dough in half. (Will make 2 Stromboli's) add 2 tbsp. of pizza sauce in the middle of dough and spread around using the back of spoon. Add 2 slices of provolone cheese, spinach, diced pepperoni, shredded chicken, half cup of Mozzarella cheese. Now fold bottom left corner to top right corner, fold bottom right corner to left top corner. Once Stromboli is closed completely turn it over and brush butter mixture on top. Cut 3 slits in the top. Place on non-stick baking dish. Place in oven on 350-375. Bake 20-25 minutes or until the dough is golden brown. When completed let Stromboli stand for 10 minutes then serve.

Cheeseburger Stew

1 lb. ground beef or ground chuck
1 green pepper diced
1 onion diced
1 can diced tomatoes drained
2 jars of garden mix salsa hot or mild
1 ½ cups of cubed sharp cheddar cheese
1 ½ tbsp. Of dried basil
1 ½ tbsp. Of dried oregano
1 tbsp. crushed red peppers (optional)
Salt and pepper to taste

In a large skillet combine ground beef or ground chuck, green pepper, onion, basil, oregano, and crushed red peppers. Cook meat until it is browned all the way through. However, while cooking meat using a spatula stir, and break meat up so that all of it cooks evenly. After meat, browns drain the access grease. Add can of diced tomatoes, both jars of salsa, and cubed cheese. Cover and reduce heat to a medium low and let simmer for 20-25 min. Every 5-8 min. stir cheeseburger mixture. Once all the cheese is melted all the way through, and bubbling then it is ready to serve. Best served over tortilla chips. Top with sour cream, sliced jalapeño's and fresh chives.

Sauté Collard Greens
with Blue Cheese Crumbles

1 sweet yellow onion chopped

6 strips of brown sugar bacon cut and diced into ½ inch pieces

½-cup blue cheese crumbles

2 bunches of collard greens

½-cup sun dried tomatoes

½ cup diced ham

1 teaspoon crushed red pepper flakes

1 tbs. Chopped garlic

In a nonstick skillet over medium heat combine onions, bacon strips, and chopped garlic. Cook until bacon browns. Drain most of the grease but leave just a little. Add collard greens, sun dried tomatoes, and diced ham. Sauté until greens are wilted down. Add blue cheese crumbles and toss lightly.

Home Made Vegetable Fried Rice

1 cup fully cooked white rice
¼ cup sesame seed oil
½ cup soy sauce
½ cup snow peas
½ diced carrots
1/3 cup minced onions
1 tbsp. Minced garlic
1 medium egg
½ cup bean sprouts

In a nonstick skillet or wok grease bottom with sesame seed oil. Let the oil get hot cooking on medium high heat. Once oil gets hot add rice, using a wooden spoon or plastic spatula stir and break up rice. Once rice start to break up add egg, snow peas, diced carrots, minced onions, and bean sprouts. Let cook till egg starts to harden, but constantly keep stirring. Once egg is cooked through slowly pour in soy sauce, constantly stir rice till it browns all the way through. Serve.

Creamed Spinach

3 strips of crumbled cooked bacon
½ heavy cream
2 tbs. Minced roasted garlic
1 tbs. Unsalted butter
1 ½ lbs. of fresh baby spinach
1 teaspoon of sea salt
1 teaspoon of fresh grind black peppercorns
½ cup shredded mozzarella cheese
¼ cup of extra virgin olive oil
1 medium sweet yellow onion chopped

In a pot heat oil and butter, add chopped onions and minced garlic. Sauté until onions are tender, add spinach in batches pushing it down to help it wilt. Keep adding spinach in pot when there is room to add. Once all the spinach is added and cooked down reduce heat, add the heavy cream, and mozzarella. Cook until cheese is melted and the sauce is thickened. Season with sea salt and black peppercorns then stir. Serve while hot and once plated grate with parmesan cheese, top with crumbled bacon.

Acknowledgements

First, I would like to thank my publishers at I universe for allowing me the opportunity to become a published author. You people helped me accomplished one of my dreams and for that I am grateful and honored to be working with you. Next I would like to thank all of my coworkers who have probably listen to me ramble on and on about countless cooking escapades and recipes or what not. Sorry, for bending your ear as often as I do but you guys have been a major inspiration to me more than you guys could ever possibly know. There is excessively many of you to list and thank personally but hopefully you know who you are. Sincerely I love and thank you guys. Next, I would like to thank Dave Rittenhouse my ride and die partner for life. Man you have been my friend, my critic, one of my biggest and most loyal supporters, and a major inspiration in your own right. For fifteen years, you have always told me the truth when everyone else would tell me what I wanted to here. Your honesty and loyalty has gone beyond measure and you are my brother from a different mother. Nevertheless, you are my blood man; I love you and thank you for your loyalty. You are much bigger than your 5'8 ¾-inch frame man. (Sorry I had to sing the song to spell your last name. Your fault though you should not have told me.) To my great grandmother Lucille O'Neal you may be gone but not all the lessons that you have instilled in me will never be forgotten. A major part of who I am is because of you. Whenever I think of you, part of me still wants to cry because I miss you so much. Since you have been gone, I have learned a lot but I still have a lot to learn. Nevertheless, in me I have your strength and desire to do so. Granny with all my heart

I love and miss you and thank you for making this family as strong as it is. You were and still are the mother to all of us. To Lucinda Curtis my mother's mother my grandma to whom I truly learned to cook from. You can out cook any TV. Chef that I watch on a daily basis, and know way more about cooking than I can ever possible hope to know. No one has gotten behind and supported, and love me more than you have. No matter what venture I was to dwell in, even if you did not understand it you were 100% on board in supporting me. One example comes to; mind like when I was a child you would watch me start at the top of hospital hill and wait for a car to approach. As soon as I would see one, I would take off running trying to beat him down the hill. (I thought I was as fast as the flash yaw, don't laugh you all did dumb things to as a youth.) Everyone in my family including my mother would say stop doing that people is going to think your retorted or something. However, not grandma she would just simply ask how many of them did you beat today baby. Well grandma I am still trying to beat the odds stacked against me and with you, riding shotgun by my side I will. Grandma I promise the next car that I chase will be the one riding towards my success, and that one I will undoubtly catch. I love you and thank you for not just making me the great cook that I am but help shaping me into the man that I am as well. To my mother Marline O'Neal who has defied the stereotype of a woman cannot raise or teach a boy to be a man. For those who think otherwise I say to you look at me and tell me do you think I'm less than any other man that you know. Growing up it was just me my mother and sister. My mother worked as hard as any man sometimes having to hold down two jobs at once just to provide for us. Back then, we did not know exactly what it took her to do the things that she did for us and often times we took it for granted. Now we are raising our own family's and have a much better understanding of how hard it must have been. I love and thank you, for all sacrifices that you made us to have the opportunities that we have today. I don't say or tell you as often as I should but I love you and thank you for all that you have provided me to face life with. To my sisters Charline, Lekeeshia, Eliza, and Marina I love you knuckle heads very much. We don't get a chance to talk as often as we would like to but when we do, it is like we haven't missed a beat. You might not know it but you guys give your big brother strength that I did not know that I had. I hope to see you all soon enough. To my brother and father to whom we all share the same first name. (That's right yaw there is three Lewis's and we're all cooks.) Bro words cannot begin to express how much I love you man. People tend to take for granted the term of keeping it 100% real. You are a million times more than that bro. You are truly a man's, man and I am proud to have you as my brother. I love you bro. Big Lewis my father motivator. Even though I did not have the opportunity to grow up around you, I have learned over the years that I am more like you than I thought. Every time that we engage in a conversation I walk away a little bit wiser and more knowledgeable about myself and how life itself work, than I did beforehand. I really don't know how to exactly tell you how much I love you or how important you are to me man. However, I think about every moment that we have been each other's company, and every conversation held within every day of my life. You have taught me more than you can ever possible know. I thank you and love you man. To my kids, Shinica, and Tyera who give daddy the wind to soar as high as I can. The love and unwavering support you girls provide me every single day can never be put into words. I know undoubtly I am a giant, cause only a giant could hold that much love in his heart that I hold for you. Watching you girls grow over the years have made my heart fill with extreme pride and joy. I can only hope that I can make you guys proud to have me as your father. To my life's partner, and the interracial reason why my heart beats deep within my soul. Tasha you are no doubt the much better half of who I am. Before you came into my life, I was lost on a journey searching for me. Once you came into my life, you helped me discover who I was and what I wanted to be. You gave me strength when I didn't feel so strong, the push and courage to pursue my goals and lifelong dreams whenever I was being apprehensive. The old saying of behind a strong man is a strong woman is wrong. Because you were never behind me, you have always been beside me as one. However, as one, it has been me and you against the world and we can't lose. There is strength in numbers and the love that we hold is much bigger than the world itself. You have stood with me when others have tried to stand on me. Each time that I felt like part of me has died on the inside; you find a way to breathe life back into me. Whenever I look in the mirror I see, you and I know that through I will live forever. I know that there is no mountain that I cannot climb, or no dragon that I cannot slay because of the love and unwavering support that is provided from you every day. To tell you that I thank you and love you for everything could not and would not be enough justice on what you have given me. I loved you then, I love you now, and I will continue to love you 1,000 eternities from now.

Printed in the United States
By Bookmasters